HAVE YOU SEEN BIRDS?

By Joanne Oppenheim

Pictures by Barbara Reid

SCHOLASTIC INC.

New York Toronto London Auckland Sydney

ISBN 0-590-40890-9

Original text copyright © 1968 by Joanne Oppenheim.
This edition text copyright © 1986 by Joanne Oppenheim.
Illustrations copyright © 1986 by Barbara Reid. All rights reserved.
This edition published by Scholastic Inc.,
730 Broadway, New York, NY 10003,
by arrangement with Scholastic-TAB Publications Ltd.

12 11 10 9 8 7 6 5 4 3   4   8 9/8 0 1 2 3/9

Printed in the U.S.A.   08

Have you seen birds?

Long-legged tall birds,

tiny bug-sized small birds,

brightly breasted,
gaily crested,
meadow tan or fancy fan.
Have you seen birds?

Have you seen spring birds?
Fluffy, cheeping,
sleeping, peeping,
ever-eating baby birds.

Or early summer garden birds?
Nesting snugly in the shrubs,
pulling worms and snapping grubs,
finding food to feed the brood,
drinking, singing,
splashing, swinging.
Have you seen birds?

Have you seen autumn birds?
Visiting-the-feeder birds,
following-the-leader birds,

leaving-in-a-string birds,
coming-back-in-spring birds.
Have you seen birds?

Have you seen winter birds?
Searching snow and tapping bark,
perching puffed in freezing dark.

Winter birds need lots of feed,
scraps of fat and sacks of seed.
Have you seen snow birds?

Have you seen woodland birds?
Lying-low shy birds,
trying-hard-to-hide birds,

Walking-upside-down birds,
acrobatic clown birds,

darting, drilling,
piping, trilling.

Listen — hear the warble
of the wild wood birds!

Whooooooo!
Have you heard the night birds?
Move-by-moonlight-bright birds,
scaring rabbits into holes,
hunting bats and rats and moles.

Have you heard the haunting *whooo*
of the hunting night-time birds?

Have you heard town birds?
Rapping-at-the-bark birds,
Cooing-in-the-park birds,

quarreling-in-a-rage birds,
tweeting-in-a-cage birds,

squealing, squawking,
screeching, talking.

Have you heard birds?

Have you seen farm birds?
Scratching, clucking,
pecking, strutting,

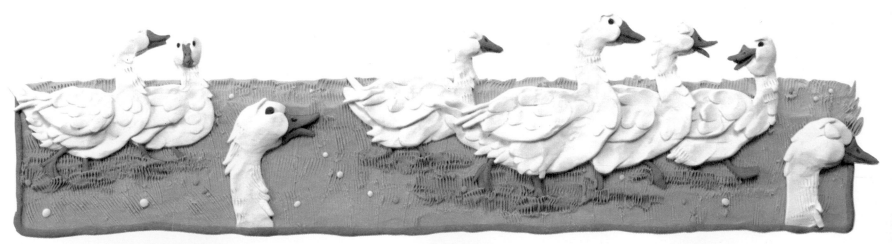

cock-a-doodle barn birds.

And on-beyond-the-barn birds —
what about the field birds?

Field-behind-the-barn birds,

cricket-catching,
berry-snatching,

whistling from a thorny thistle.
Have you seen birds?

Have you seen marsh birds?
Webfoot, paddling water birds,
walking-with-a-waddle birds,

wading in the reeds.

Do you know sea birds?
Twisting, drifting,
swiftly shifting,

searching, skimming,
scooping, lifting,
soaring by the shore.

Or flat-footed fishing birds,
fussing, chatting,
flipper-flapping,
diving for their food.

Have you seen these birds?

Look up — see the sky birds,
flying-way-up-high birds,
racing-up-to-space birds,

wind-wheeling,
freedom-feeling,
diving, dipping,
gliding, tipping.
Have you seen birds?

A band, a flight,
a flock of birds —
the world is full of
lots of birds!

Have you seen birds?